Financial Due Diligence

Pearson Education

In an increasingly competitive world, it is quality of thinking that gives an edge – an idea that opens new doors, a technique that solves a problem, or an insight that simply helps make sense of it all.

We work with leading authors in the fields of management and finance to bring cutting-edge thinking and best learning practice to a global market.

Under a range of leading imprints, including *Financial Times Prentice Hall*, we create world-class print publications and electronic products giving readers knowledge and understanding which can be applied, whether studying or at work.

To find out more about our business and professional products, you can visit us at www.business-minds.com

For other Pearson Education publications, visit www.pearsoned-ema.com

MANAGEMENT BRIEFINGS
EXECUTIVE BRIEFING

Financial Due Diligence

A Guide to Ensuring Successful Acquisitions

STEPHEN BOURNE

FINANCIAL TIMES
Prentice Hall

London	New York	San Francisco	Toronto	Sydney
Tokyo	Singapore	Hong Kong	Cape Town	Madrid
Paris	Milan	Munich	Amsterdam	

PEARSON EDUCATION LIMITED

Head Office:
Edinburgh Gate
Harlow CM20 2JE
Tel: +44 (0)1279 623623
Fax: +44 (0)1279 431059

London Office:
128 Long Acre, London WC2E 9AN
Tel: +44 (0)207 447 2000
Fax: +44 (0)207 240 5771
Website: www.business-minds.com

First published in Great Britain in 2000

ISBN 0 273 64224 3

British Library Cataloguing in Publication Data
A CIP catalogue record for this book can be obtained from the British Library.

10 9 8 7 6 5 4 3 2 1

Typeset by Boyd Elliott Typesetting
Printed and bound in Great Britain

The Publishers' policy is to use paper manufactured from sustainable forests.

About the author

Stephen Bourne is the London lead partner at BDO Stoy Hayward Corporate Finance.

Stephen studied English Literature at Reading University before joining Pannell Kerr Forster in 1978. In 1983, two years after qualifying as a chartered accountant, he transferred to the corporate finance department, becoming a partner in 1988. He subsequently became National Director of Corporate Finance before leaving to join BDO Stoy Hayward in 1997. He was appointed lead corporate finance partner in 1998 and sits on BDO's national and international corporate finance committees.

Stephen has advised a wide range of public and private companies on over 200 UK and international acquisitions over the last 16 years. While at PKF he developed a comprehensive corporate finance manual and is the author of BDO's internal investigations guideline. Stephen is a regular conference speaker on the subject of financial due diligence.

BDO Stoy Hayward Corporate Finance

BDO Stoy Hayward Corporate Finance is a rapidly growing adviser to entrepreneurial public and private companies. With around 50 corporate finance staff at the Central London office, additional specialists in a number of offices in the Home Counties and corporate finance departments in major regional centres, BDO advises on all aspects of corporate transactions, including the following:

- acquiring public and private companies;
- selling businesses;
- raising private equity;
- strategic reviews;
- investigating investment targets;
- reporting on flotations, rights issues and material acquisitions by PLCs.

Stephen may be contacted at:

BDO Stoy Hayward Corporate Finance
8 Baker Street
London W1M 1DA

Tel: +44 (0)207 486 5888
Fax: +44 (0)207 487 3686
Web site: www.bdo.co.uk

Contents

Introduction

According to *Acquisitions Monthly*, in 1992 there were 629 sales of private companies in the UK: six years later the number had more than doubled to 1298. Over the same period the annual number of divestments of businesses by UK public limited companies (PLCs) increased from 468 to 798. When some 400 management buyouts per annum are taken into account, over 2500 transactions were completed by UK companies in 1998. Corporate acquisitions are now undeniably a fundamental part of business life in the UK and a cornerstone of most strategic plans which target rapid growth.

So who are the acquisitive companies buying so many other businesses every year? Well, they come in all shapes and sizes, from entrepreneurs making their first bolt-on acquisition, to the established family company extending the geographical reach of its operations, to smaller quoted companies consolidating fragmented industries, to larger quoted companies strengthening their grip on a particular market or diversifying into related, or sometimes unrelated, areas, to venture capitalists, to overseas companies moving into the UK for the first time.

And who are the companies being acquired? They primarily fall into two categories: first, privately owned businesses, frequently owner-managed and established either by the current directors or previous family generations. For these companies, the time has come, for whatever reason, to realise the capital value of the business. The second category is corporately owned businesses, no longer regarded as core activities by current management, usually as a result of a change in strategic direction.

The fact is that there is now an active marketplace in UK businesses and there is no sign that it will contract in the foreseeable future. Many senior managers will consequently find themselves effecting acquisitions for the first time or on an infrequent basis. Given the diversity of situations that arise during the acquisition process, even those with previous experience will constantly see new situations, come across a variety of levels of access to data and have to work within a range of timescales.

In addition, practices surrounding the sale of businesses develop and change over time. As an example of one such change, it is now quite common for the vendor to commission an independent financial due diligence report which is shown to a short list of potential buyers and eventually 'signed over' to the successful buyer. This prevents the acquiror appointing the investigating accountants of its choice and gives greater control over the sale process to the vendor. How should an acquiror react if this is suggested? Should an acquiror supplement such a report with its own investigations? Who should pay for a 'vendor due diligence' report?

The purpose of this briefing is to answer many of these types of questions by giving guidance to both financial and non-financial senior management on the following:

- the key financial due diligence issues to focus upon;
- the key questions to be answered;
- how to instruct investigating accountants;
- how they will typically go about their work;
- what can be expected from them;
- the types of issues that arise during the financial investigation;
- how financial due diligence interacts with other parts of the acquisition process.

Although this briefing is not intended to be a manual setting out how to undertake a financial due diligence review, it inevitably sets out many of the key issues that need to be addressed during the process. It can therefore be used as a comprehensive checklist to assist in the process of instructing investigating accountants and against which their work can be assessed.

In particular, each of Chapters 5 to 13 of this briefing considers an area typically covered by financial due diligence. The format of all those chapters is similar in that they primarily comprise checklists of key questions to be answered and issues to be included in the financial due diligence report, together with brief case studies illustrating the findings of actual investigations.

No two investigations are the same and it is not possible to define a scope of due diligence review or report format that is appropriate in all instances. There can never be a substitute for experience and the flexibility of mind that a good investigating accountant must bring to an assignment. This briefing should, however, demystify the financial due diligence process and take some of the stress out of the process for those who are not involved in financial due diligence on a full-time basis.

Objectives of financial due diligence

FACTORS AFFECTING OBJECTIVES

The specific objectives of any financial due diligence exercise will vary depending upon factors such as:

- the complexity of the business;
- the extent of the acquiror's existing knowledge of the business;
- the extent of access to the target given to the acquiror;
- the degree of access given to the investigating accountants;
- the materiality of the acquisition;
- the fullness of the price.

Where the target is a relatively small business which replicates the acquiror's existing operations (e.g. a large group of motor dealerships acquiring a further franchise, or a nursing home group buying another home) the objectives of financial due diligence can be fairly limited. Alternatively, a target that will double the size of the acquiror's business, is multi-site or activity, is in a new market or industry or is priced on a high earnings multiple, is likely to be the subject of more extensive financial due diligence.

STAGES OF AN ACQUISITION

Before considering the objectives of financial due diligence in detail, it is worth noting the point in the overall acquisition process at which financial due diligence is undertaken. The broad stages of the acquisition process are summarised in Table 2.1.

Table 2.1 Stages of the acquisition process

Stage	Comment
Develop an acquisition strategy	If serious about acquiring, then careful consideration of acquisition criteria will save time and money. Focus on the ideal in terms of size, products, markets, geographical location. Decide how to finance the deal once agreed. Line up legal, financial and commercial advisers. Select methods of sourcing acquisitions. Form a view on valuation approach. Allocate internal responsibility for implementing the strategy.
Identify targets	Circulating acquisition criteria to firms of accountants, business brokers, lawyers, financial advisers, etc. will get so far. Going to see them and making personal contacts will go one step further.

But this is essentially a passive way of finding suitable acquisition targets and, even if it is successful, there will be competition to buy a company that is being actively marketed. This drives up the price and reduces the chance of a completion. Do not wait for people to offer opportunities. Using either in-house resources or professional advisers, search for and research companies that meet the chosen acquisition criteria and identify them before they are being offered for sale.

Making the approach

Depending on the circumstances, accountants could be used to make the first contact with the target. In this way anonymity is initially maintained, the target believes the approach is serious and a financial adviser is involved from the earliest stages. In any event, the approach should preferably be via the telephone rather than in writing, and care should be taken to ensure that the right person is contacted. Remember that a managing director who is not a major shareholder may not always have a vested interest in forwarding details of the approach to the principal owners of the company.

Initial review

Once an interest in selling the business has been confirmed, there will be some form of initial review. This may include any or all of the following:

■ independent research;
■ in-house commercial knowledge;
■ statutory accounts and filings at Companies House;
■ an information memorandum and/or access to a 'data-room' (if the business is being professionally marketed);
■ information given verbally at meetings;
■ selected papers provided by the target.

Whether on the basis of fairly detailed information or just a few key figures and a broad understanding of market position, a view on valuation will be formed and an offer made.

Heads of agreement

The heads of agreement summarise the principal terms of the offer agreed between the acquiror and the vendor. It will typically be two to six pages long and not legally binding. A well-drafted heads will avoid misunderstandings on key issues later in the process. It will also provide the acquiror with a period of exclusivity in which to carry out due diligence and complete the transaction. Both legal and financial advisers should be involved in its drafting.

Due diligence	This is the point at which significant fees start to be incurred with a range of professional advisers. The different due diligence areas can include any or all of the following, depending upon the nature of the target's operations: ■ financial; ■ commercial; ■ tax; ■ legal; ■ property; ■ environmental; ■ pensions; ■ information technology.
Negotiating completion	Following the receipt of the various due diligence reports there may be a renegotiation of the principal terms or the deal structure. The detailed warranties in the purchase contract will need to be negotiated, as will directors' service contracts, incentive schemes, etc.

Following completion there is the further process stage of integrating the acquisition with existing operations, a frequently challenging task that rarely goes as smoothly as anticipated. There may also be periodic work over a number of years relating to the determination of the final consideration. Many transactions, for example, require a certain level of net asset value to be provided at the completion date and this can only be confirmed some months later following a completion audit of the target. In addition, the auditors may be required to 'certify' in an agreed form the profits of the target for the next one to five years in order to help determine the amount of consideration payable under 'earn-out' arrangements.

OBJECTIVES

The key point to note from Table 2.1 is that financial due diligence commences after a price has been agreed for the business (subject to contract and satisfactory due diligence). Up to that point the vendor has controlled the flow of information to the acquiror, restricting access to prime documentation and providing facts and figures which are naturally aimed at portraying the business in the best possible light. It is rare indeed for a vendor to disclose at this stage that its financial systems are inadequate, that it has lost major customers, that its selling prices are under severe pressure, that staff turnover is high, that a key salesperson has resigned, that it has recently changed its accounting practices to report profits earlier, that one non-recurring exceptional contract accounted for most of its profits last year, that it has major lease dilapidation liabilities, etc., etc.

An acquiror will usually have formed initial views on a range of issues before deciding to make an offer, including matters such as:

- has the target got a good reputation in its industry;
- does it have attractive products, services and market positions;
- is its customer base desirable;
- has it got a good management team;
- what is its 'maintainable profit' level;
- what is the value of its net assets;
- is it cash generative;
- does it appear to have a good future?

Fundamental to the acquiror's view of the price that it is willing to pay is the profit record of the target. The offer will have been arrived at on the basis of historical, current and budgeted profitability, and an assumption that there are no unrecorded actual or contingent liabilities that may impact adversely on future profitability. **The principal objective of financial due diligence, therefore, is usually to look behind the initial information provided by the target and to assist the acquiror in forming a view on the level of *'maintainable profit'*.**

'Maintainable profit' is that level of annual profit which the acquiror reasonably believes the target is capable of earning on an ongoing basis. Its assessment involves reviewing historical profits and adjusting them for exceptional items; considering current reported profits, the means by which they are generated and the reliability of the information systems which calculate them; and reviewing budgets and the detailed assumptions behind them.

At the time an offer is made it is usually impossible for an acquiror to achieve the above on the basis of its own detailed review. The target's representations are accepted in good faith. The investigating accountant's role is thoroughly to test those representations. An understanding of the business is essential to a proper understanding of the financial information, and the investigating accountant, as we shall see later, usually considers operational as well as purely financial issues.

In order to achieve its principal objective, the financial due diligence process can have any or all of the following objectives for individual areas of the investigation:

- to provide a brief description of the history of the business, including key events in its development, and to comment upon its markets, competitors, customers, products/services, methods of production/service delivery, suppliers and overall mode of operation;
- to summarise details of management structure and senior managers, together with the key characteristics of the workforce, highlighting strengths, weaknesses and constraining factors therein;

- to consider the acceptability of key accounting policies and practices, and provide an overview of the substance and adequacy of management information systems;

- to explain and comment on the significant factors behind the reported trading results for recent years and any exceptional or non-recurring items which have had a material impact thereon;

- to explain and comment on the assets and liabilities of the business and, in particular, to consider valuation bases and the basis of recognising liabilities;

- to summarise recent cash flow patterns and the significant factors affecting them;

- to summarise details of the current status of the tax affairs of the business;

- to comment on management's trading and cash flow projections, the method of compilation, and key underlying assumptions, with particular reference to their relationship with current trading levels.

In addition to the above, it may be convenient for the investigating accountant to gather and summarise within the report certain sundry information on the target, e.g. details of property leases, insurance cover and future capital commitments. There is a risk that this may constitute a duplication of work done by the acquiror's legal advisers. However, the advantage of including brief summaries of such items in the financial due diligence report is that the report begins to be an overall profile of the target. This is particularly useful when information on the acquisition has to be passed to senior management or non-executive directors who are not directly involved in managing the acquisition process.

If the right objectives are set and then met, the resultant investigation work should significantly assist the acquiror to decide whether it wants to confirm or revise its original offer, what terms might be appropriate, whether the proposed transaction should proceed and, in certain areas, what needs to be done post-completion to integrate the target.

Instructing investigating accountants

It is vital that an acquiror properly instructs appropriate investigating accountants. Failure to do so will result in poor or incomplete due diligence, lack of co-ordination between the acquiror's team of advisers, delays, cost inefficiencies, deals being completed at too high a price or, in the worst cases, deals being completed that should not have been completed at all, and insufficient protection being built into the warranties in the sale agreement.

SELECTING

Although the investigating process has a methodology to it, it is not as regimented and structured as the audit process. Due diligence work requires flexibility, inquisitiveness and a greater degree of knowledge and experience than most audit work. There is an increased emphasis on analysis of data, interviewing skills, appraising people and communicating detailed findings. While some auditors comfortably make the transition, others do not.

If you have a good working relationship with your auditors then that should be your starting point. Most major firms of accountants have due diligence specialists in their Investigations or Corporate Finance departments, although some prefer to service financial due diligence out of their audit groups. Although the reputation of the firm is important, the individual qualities of the team are paramount. You need to feel that you will receive good advice and a committed service from those individuals, that you will matter to them and that you can work with them through a stressful and demanding period. Take the time to discuss the deal, its pricing, your strategy, how your advisers should work as a team, the timetable and the scope of the work. Consider obtaining recommendations from your bankers or lawyers, but be sure to ask why a particular individual is being recommended.

Cost is bound to be an important consideration and can vary significantly from firm to firm. Most firms will base their fee estimate on budgeted hours for each member of the team, charged out at an hourly rate, and they should be willing to share this budget with you. It is extremely difficult to accurately estimate the time needed to complete a financial due diligence exercise, primarily because the degree of co-operation and level of organisation of the target are unknown until the work commences. Factors such as poor accounting systems, poor audit files, lack of availability of senior management and delays in meeting information requests all add to the time and cost of an investigation.

There are three basic options for the fee basis agreed with investigating accountants:

1 time incurred charged at normal hourly rates;

2 a fixed fee for a specified schedule of work;

3 either of the above with the fee subject to a discount if the deal aborts and an uplift if it succeeds.

Option 1 should always be accompanied by an estimate of the range in which fees are expected to fall (e.g. £50 000 to £60 000) and an agreement that any likely overrun against the estimate should be brought to the acquiror's attention immediately with a view to agreeing a higher range.

Option 2 involves a degree of risk for the investigating accountant and may result in a higher fee than option 1.

Option 3 has become increasingly common in recent years as acquirors seek to minimise their costs in the event that the transaction does not complete. This option is particularly popular among financial buyers such as venture capitalists. The range of discounts that can be negotiated is typically from 20 per cent to 30 per cent, although larger discounts are occasionally offered. The impact on fees can be significant, as demonstrated in Fig. 3.1.

Fig. 3.1   **Example of impact of abort fee arrangements**

	£'000
Estimated time costs	100
Abort fee with 30% discount	70
Success fee with 30% uplift	130

The major difficulty with such 'contingent fee' arrangements is the perceived or actual risk to independent and frank reporting of the findings of the investigation. In the example in Fig. 3.1, the investigating accountants' abort fees are almost doubled if the deal is completed: at a 50 per cent discount level the success fee would be three times the abort fee. Although superficially attractive, therefore, heavily contingent fees may consciously or subconsciously lead to negative findings or opinions being watered down. Most investigating accountants will wish to remove any impression of a lack of independence arising from their fee arrangements by keeping abort fees within reasonable limits.

Whatever fee basis is agreed, be prepared to pay fees which appear high in relation to audit fees. There is little scope when undertaking a due diligence review to utilise the trainee accountants who comprise the majority of most audit teams. Most of the team will be qualified accountants and significant input is required from senior personnel.

One of the most contentious issues surrounding the appointment of investigating accountants is the 'limitation of liability' clauses which many firms insert into their engagement letters. These clauses tend to limit the amount of damages that can be claimed against the investigating accountant in the event of

negligence. The limit might be set at a multiple of fees, say ten times, or at an absolute limit which varies dependent upon the deal size.

While accountants would argue that some limitation is only reasonable in view of their unlimited status and personal exposure, acquirors quite understandably query why they should accept a cap which might not cover the losses that they could incur through the accountant's negligence. If the job is done properly, the investigating accountant has nothing to worry about; if it is not, then surely the client should be fully compensated.

While some firms would concur with the above, and do not impose limitations of liability clauses, others have an entrenched view and will not undertake financial due diligence work without a liability cap being agreed. Before accepting a liability cap an acquiror should obtain a full explanation of why it is there, and not simply accept that it is 'our firm's policy'. It may be appropriate to ask about the recent claims record of the firm if faced with an inflexible attitude on this issue.

In order to assist the process of selecting investigating accountants, a checklist of points to consider is set out in Fig. 3.2.

Fig. 3.2   Dos and Don'ts of selecting investigating accountants

Do

As a minimum meet the team member who will lead the on-site work and, if practical, meet the whole team.

Meet the partners, discuss their investigations experience and the extent of their planned involvement.

Discuss industry experience.

Ask for views on the price that you have agreed to pay for the company.

Ask about the nature of the report that you will receive.

Consider asking for references.

If in doubt, interview a second firm.

Don't

Let the investigating accountant dictate the scope of work to you.

Select a firm without meeting the individuals.

Instruct a firm after meeting a 'sales team' rather than the service team.

Make a choice on the basis of price alone.

Accept 'limitation of liability' clauses without a full and satisfactory explanation of why they are needed.

SCOPING

The scope of financial due diligence can range from a limited review for one person for several days to teams of people in a number of locations for over a month. If a full scope investigation is undertaken, the contents of the financial due diligence report should be similar to that suggested in Fig. 3.3.

Fig. 3.3 Contents of a financial due diligence report

> **CONTENTS**
> 1   Introduction
> 2   Summary of findings
> 3   History and commercial activities
> 4   Organisational structure and employees
> 5   Accounting policies and information systems
> 6   Trading results
> 7   Net assets
> 8   Taxation
> 9   Cash flows
> 10 Financial projections
> 11 Other matters

It is important to define as closely as possible the underlying work that the acquiror requires to be done under each heading. To assist this process, most investigating accountants will have a detailed listing of the suggested scope of an investigation which will be attached as an appendix to their engagement letter. A typical example is set out in Fig. 3.4.

Fig. 3.4 Scope of financial due diligence

1	**INTRODUCTION**
2	**SUMMARY OF FINDINGS**
3	**HISTORY AND COMMERCIAL ACTIVITIES**
3.1	History and development of the Group and the activities undertaken.
3.2	The corporate structure of the Group.
3.3	A description of the Group's activities and its commercial objectives and policies.

3.4 A breakdown of turnover by categories for the last three years.

3.5 An assessment (where possible) of the size and development of the principal markets in which the Group operates, its main customer type, potential customers and assessment of market share.

3.6 Details of the Group's relationships with suppliers, an assessment of the relative importance of each major source of supply and details of any particular commercial relationships.

3.7 Details of how the Group finances its activities. Details of any special financial arrangements.

3.8 Details of any new activities planned, recently commenced or terminated.

3.9 Details of trade associations, bonding arrangements, etc.

3.10 Details of the activities of and relationship with any other companies owned by, or in which an interest is held by, the shareholders or directors of the Company, having a trading or other relationship with the Group.

3.11 An assessment of the Group's vulnerability to changes in market conditions, interest rates and any other significant factors.

3.12 Details of the Group's properties including location, form and terms of tenure, current usage, date of acquisition, cost and current valuation.

3.13 Details of planned future expenditure on the above properties.

3.14 A schedule of the net book values of the properties. (A professional open-market valuation of the properties may be undertaken by a firm of chartered surveyors and valuers.)

3.15 In the case of any let properties, details of tenants, terms of lease, rental income etc.

4 ORGANISATIONAL STRUCTURE AND EMPLOYEES

4.1 Management structure.

4.2 Details of the directors and senior management, terms of employment including details of service contracts, bonus or commission payable, pensions, benefits, loans and expenses, if applicable. Commentary on changes planned in the context of the proposed acquisition.

4.3 Assessment of management succession.

4.4   Broad details of the workforce including terms of employment, numbers, remuneration policy and staff relations, noting trades unions that are recognised.

4.5   Availability of staff, recruitment policy and training.

4.6   Dates of salary/wage reviews and current status of such.

4.7   Details of profit sharing and bonus schemes.

4.8   Details of pension schemes and indication of funding position.

4.9   Summary of any important relationships with outside contractors and professional advisers and the extent of the Group's reliance upon them.

5   ACCOUNTING POLICIES AND INFORMATION SYSTEMS

5.1   A statement of accounting policies adopted by the Group, details of any changes in policy during the review period.

5.2   A description and assessment of the financial records produced by the Group and the systems of internal control and a comparison with the acquiror's policies.

5.3   A description and assessment of the costing systems and the budgetary control and forecasting systems.

5.4   A description and assessment of the management information produced by the Group including an assessment of auditors' management letters.

6   TRADING RESULTS

6.1   A summary of the consolidated results of the Group covering the three-year period ended <<PERIODENDEDDATE1>> ('the review period').

6.2   A breakdown of gross profit analysed by each main activity for the review period together with an explanation as to significant variations.

6.3   A statement of adjustments to be made to the profit and loss accounts and balance sheets over the review period to reflect consistent accounting policies or the impact of exceptional items.

6.4   An analysis of overhead expenses together with comments on significant fluctuations.

6.5   An explanation of the major fluctuations in turnover and profits during the review period.

6.6   An explanation of and comments on trends disclosed by the results to include relevant notes of any exceptional profits or losses and any other significant contributory factors.

7   NET ASSETS

7.1   A summary statement of the consolidated balance sheets of the Group as at <<A&LDATE>> and <<PERIODENDEDDATE1>>.

7.2   An analysis of/comments on the main assets and liabilities of the Group as at <<PERIODENDEDDATE1>>.

7.3   Details of any material long-term and/or onerous contracts.

7.4   Details of banking facilities available to the Group, including covenants and any onerous conditions, breaches and renewal dates.

7.5   Details of the Group's capital structure.

8   TAXATION

8.1   Details of the current position with regard to the agreement of taxation liabilities, deferred taxation, shortfall clearances and assessments.

8.2   Details of any unusual pay as you earn (PAYE) or value added tax (VAT) practices and the findings of the last inspections of these areas.

9   CASH FLOWS

9.1   A statement of the Group's cash flows covering the three-year period ended <<PERIODENDEDDATE1>>.

9.2   A commentary on the Group's ability to generate cash on the basis of the above.

10   FINANCIAL PROJECTIONS

10.1   A review of the profit and cash flow projections of the Group for the period ending <<PERIODENDEDDATE2>>, including the following:

- consideration of the method of preparation;
- a review of the projections' arithmetical accuracy;
- a review of the commercial assumptions made by the directors and comments upon any assumptions that appear unrealistic;
- a review of cash flow projections against borrowing facilities;
- a sensitivity analysis of the projections in relation to the key assumptions upon which they have been prepared.

11   OTHER MATTERS

11.1   Details of any current, pending or threatened litigation or legal proceedings against or involving the Group.

11.2   Details of any contingent liabilities.

11.3   Details of the Group's insurance cover.

Such a contents list should be reviewed line by line and amended to delete items not required and to add items of particular interest. Give as much guidance as possible on the relative importance of each area, the depth of investigation required and the detail needed in the due diligence report. A few extra hours spent getting the scope right, and as specific as possible, will be time well spent. When an acquisition is being funded by loan finance the financiers should be consulted on scope to ensure that it meets their requirements. It is important to remember that the scope should be revisited at regular intervals throughout the due diligence process and modified in light of findings to date and changes in circumstances.

More limited investigations tend to reduce the work on the history and commercial activities of the company, organisational structure and employees, and accounting systems. This is usually because the details are already known to the acquiror or are not material to the investment decision. Alternatively, it may be that they are so material that specialist commercial, human resources or information technology consultants have been separately instructed. Even in cases where the scope is reduced to a purely financial review, it is vital that the investigating team spends time understanding the target business, including its products, markets, positioning and operating structure.

In circumstances where due diligence is being restricted by the vendor to a review of selected information placed in a dataroom, the scope of the review initially will be severely restricted. The acquiror should establish the degree of access that will be granted to the successful bidder after the auction process and seek to negotiate full direct access to financial records and managers. If such access is denied it may be appropriate to withdraw from the process rather than incur costs on an exercise that cannot give the necessary level of comfort.

Alternatively, the vendor may intend to provide a 'vendor due diligence report' to the successful bidder, or final short list of bidders. This is a due diligence report by an independent firm of investigating accountants that is commissioned by the vendor on the understanding that the accountants will address it to the successful bidder and owe them a duty of care. The acquiror may be asked to pay the costs of the investigating accountants in return for access to the report.

Such reports are increasingly common when businesses with a value in excess of £10 million are being systematically marketed. They are of less value than a report prepared by the acquiror's investigating accountants as:

1 the report will have been vetted by the vendor prior to release and any criticisms inevitably toned down;

2 the acquiror will not have directed the scope of the report and will have had no input to the process;

3 generally, there will be few opinions and more analysis of figures without explanatory commentary;

4 they are frequently prepared by the vendor's auditors and are unlikely, therefore, to highlight any deficiencies in past audits or acceptance by them of contentious accounting practices;

5 the acquiror will not have had oral feedback from the investigating accountant on general impressions or specific issues that are not in the initially set scope.

Notwithstanding the above, if an attractive business is being marketed and the vendor due diligence route is chosen, then acquirors have little choice but to accept its limitations. What they can do, however, is insist on two things:

■ first, a meeting with the investigating accountant's team to discuss the report and any other issues;

■ second, the right to issue further instructions to 'top up' the scope of the report.

Particular difficulties can emerge when attempting to scope the work needed in relation to overseas businesses. Accounting and tax practices differ considerably from country to country, as does the extent to which financial due diligence is customarily undertaken. In general, a UK-style financial due diligence review is more comprehensive than that found in other parts of the world. It is essential that the investigating accountants liaise with his or her local office at an early stage and that a clear explanation of the acquiror's requirements is given. In order to ensure that a UK reporting style and format are adopted it may be appropriate to have someone from the UK leading and co-ordinating a local team. The cost implications of such an approach are usually not material when compared with the additional comfort that this can give.

ENGAGEMENT LETTERS

The scope and terms of the financial due diligence should be confirmed as early as is practicable in an engagement letter. The letter will typically cover:

■ the addressees of the due diligence report;

- the scope of the review;
- areas specifically excluded from the review;
- the reporting timetable;
- the person responsible for the work;
- fee arrangements;
- any agreed liability cap.

The engagement letter may also contain clauses which limit the distribution of the resultant report, emphasise that no audit work will be done or warn that trading projections must be regarded with caution. Some firms have more than a dozen pages of detailed terms and conditions of business attached to their engagement letters. A typical engagement letter, without the detailed terms and conditions, is set out in Fig. 3.5.

Fig. 3.5   **Financial due diligence engagement letter**

Address of Directors

Date

Dear Sirs

XX Limited ('XX' or 'the Company') – Proposed acquisition of the net assets of the OO plc ('OO')

We are writing to confirm our understanding of your instructions to us in connection with the above and to request formal instructions to carry out the work stipulated below.

1   **Accountants' Presentation and Report**

1.1   We will prepare a detailed presentation on the items listed in the appendix to this letter, together with any other matters which come to our attention in the course of our work and which we consider should be brought to your attention in the context of our instructions. The presentation will be supported by a full set of relevant appendices and will be followed by a summary report which will include a summary of key findings, conclusions and recommendations.

1.2   Our procedures in preparing the presentation and report will not comprise an audit and we will not be in a position to express a formal opinion on the financial information which we will be reviewing.

2 **Taxation**

2.1 We will carry out a review of the taxation matters of the Company and the implications on XX of the proposed acquisition of OO.

3 **Other Matters**

3.1 We will liaise as required with you and your other professional advisers in respect of the financial and commercial implications arising from the proposed acquisition of OO.

3.2 We would hope to start our work on dd/mm/yy and, on the basis of our current knowledge of the assignment, would expect that we will be in a position to report our findings in the form of a presentation to you on dd/mm/yy. Our summary report is likely to be issued on dd/mm/yy.

3.3 Our fees are based upon the time necessarily spent using the appropriate grade of staff. Assuming that no unforeseen problems arise during the course of the assignment and that the above timetable is met, we estimate a fee for this work of approximately £ (excluding expenses and VAT). A final bill will be sent to XX Limited on submission of the final report and payment is required within 14 days.

3.4 If the transaction aborts, for whatever reason, prior to completion, then a fee will be raised equivalent to our time costs outstanding at the date the transaction is aborted. Under these circumstances, a bill will be sent to XX Limited as soon as is practicable and payment will be required within 14 days.

4 **Complaints**

4.1 If at any time you would like to discuss with us how our service to you could be improved, or if you are dissatisfied with any aspect of the service you are receiving, please let us know by contacting the firm's senior partner.

4.2 We undertake to look into any complaint carefully and promptly. In the event that you are not satisfied with the resolution of any complaint you may raise with us, then you have the right to report the matter to the Institute of Chartered Accountants in England and Wales.

4.3   In the event of any dispute arising in respect of or relating to the services to be provided in accordance with this letter or any additional services to be provided by us such dispute shall be determined by the exclusive jurisdiction of the English courts.

Please confirm that we have correctly understood your requirements and that you agree to the terms of our engagement by signing and returning the enclosed copy of this letter to us.

Yours faithfully

The engagement letter will be used as a checklist by the investigating accountant throughout the investigation. It is essential that it is revisited periodically to ensure that it is supplemented to take account of changes in circumstances, such as timetable delays, a need to expand or contract the scope, cost over-runs or additional addressees to the due diligence report.

Most reporting accountants will wish to issue their own engagement letter rather than receive one from their client. Ensure that you are satisfied that it fully reflects the range of discussions that you will have held and that there are no overly onerous restrictions on the use to which you may put the report.

REPORTING FORMATS

The traditional financial due diligence report tends to comprise a long and detailed report, anything in length from 50 to 150 pages, with a large volume of appendices. In some circumstances a tremendous amount of detail is required, either because of the culture of the organisation commissioning the work or the need to fully inform non-executive directors or parent company boards of a transaction that they are remote from. Alternatively, certain acquirors take the approach that, while they want a thorough underlying investigation, they want only material issues brought to their attention in a written report. Such a report might be restricted to, say, 20 or 30 pages, with a more limited volume of appendices being attached as a result of data such as asset listings, employee details and legal agreements being omitted. This can significantly reduce the cost of financial due diligence.

A third option is for an acquiror to request a presentation of the results of the investigation to be made. This will usually involve an on-screen presentation using PowerPoint or equivalent software, accompanied by hard copies of the slides with space below each slide for notes to be made. This option is sometimes selected by

experienced acquirors undertaking a transaction that is not particularly material to them. It is also an excellent method of reporting the draft findings of an investigation in advance of the detailed report having been fully written. It is interesting to note that venture capitalists frequently request such a presentation.

Certain investigating accountants have very rigid ideas, or even internal rules, which will determine the format in which they report. Most of these formats will be completely acceptable to the majority of acquirors, and presentational standards have improved considerably in recent years. The use of graphics, for example, is now widespread and can be very effective in communicating key issues or data succinctly. Some firms, however, adopt a reporting style that comprises a long series of '*bullet points*' which are then talked about and expanded upon. Although this is a concise style, it may cause difficulties in that the recipient is forced to annotate the report with supporting details. It is also less useful for circulating to parties who did not attend the discussions on the report. This will not suit all acquirors.

Each acquiror needs to give careful thought to its preferred reporting format, which may vary from acquisition to acquisition, depending upon prevailing circumstances. This should then be discussed with the investigating accountants and a fairly clear indication of expectations should be given. If there is any resistance or uncertainty in these discussions, it is worth asking to see previous examples of reports prepared by the investigating accountants. This will enable an acquiror to select those presentational elements that it likes and make clear what it does not like.

4

Starting and controlling the investigation

BRIEFING

Too many financial due diligence investigations start with an inadequate briefing for the investigating accountant by the acquiror. Information about both the target and the rationale for the transaction should be given to the investigating accountant at the first briefing meeting. Issues to be covered are set out in Fig. 4.1.

Fig. 4.1 Briefing checklist

Points for discussion:

- history of the transaction so far;
- outline of the deal;
- valuation methodology of the acquiror;
- strategic rationale for undertaking the transaction;
- funding proposals;
- interaction of the acquiror's advisers and respective roles;
- key issues for the acquiror;
- scope of the financial due diligence;
- interim feedback/report arrangements;
- format of final report;
- timetable;
- confidential communication lines.

Information to be provided:

- heads of agreement;
- accounts of target;
- information memorandum;
- research/background material;
- internal reports on the proposed transaction;
- names and addresses of target and its advisers;
- names and addresses of acquiror contacts and its advisers.

Following the briefing, the investigating accountant should understand how the acquiror sourced the transaction, why it wants to do the deal, how the price was justified, what are the key valuation issues, how much background work the acquiror has done, how much financial due diligence is required and what is the preferred reporting format. The investigating accountant will further know who is aware of the proposed transaction, who the other professional advisers are on both sides, the time available in which to do the work and who to contact to start the investigation.

The nature of the target's operations and the required scope of work will determine the team size and allow a costing to be prepared. The majority of investigations take three to five weeks to get to the first draft report stage, although multi-site investigations, restrictions upon access to the target or ill-prepared/uncooperative target management can protract the timetable considerably. It is impossible to predict how well prepared a target is or what issues will arise during the investigation to slow down the process. Acquirors should start with a realistic timetable which applies reasonable pressure on all parties, but be prepared for the almost inevitable slippage that occurs during the transaction.

The briefing stage should also include a meeting between the principal advisers, particularly the lawyers and accountants, but also specialist consultants when involved. This will avoid duplications of information requests and enable a direct dialogue on issues as the transaction progresses.

A thorough briefing accompanied by initial reading material will enable the investigating accountant to plan work and review relevant data before starting on site.

HOLD HARMLESS LETTERS

Most of the investigative work will be done at the target's premises or, in the latter stages, at the investigating accountant's office. However, a visit to the target's auditors forms a vital element of the early stages of an investigation. The last two or three years' audit files will usually be reviewed, together with corporation tax files for up to six years. This review can often provide the following information:

- accounting analyses of sales, fixed assets, stock, debtors, etc.;
- explanations of year on year movements in sales, gross margins and overheads;
- details of accounting policies and practices, and in particular comments on those that are contentious;
- comments on the quality of the accounting systems;
- an indication of the accuracy of management accounts figures.

Most importantly, it is only by reviewing the audit files that the investigating accountant can form a view on the overall quality of the audit and the extent, therefore, to which balance sheet and profit and loss account figures have been subjected to detailed scrutiny. The extent to which detailed testing occurs during an audit can vary significantly. Where the target business is part of a large group it may not have been visited at all in recent years by the group auditors. Similarly, audit work can be somewhat less than expected when the auditors are relied upon by the target to prepare its monthly and/or annual financial statements. It cannot

be assumed, therefore, that the presence of a signed audit report means that the financial statements have always been subjected to detailed scrutiny.

A 'hold harmless' letter will usually be issued by the target's auditors before the investigating accountants are allowed access to their working papers. The letter is signed by both the investigating accountants and the acquiror. It explains that the audit working papers may not be relied upon by the investigating accountants and that the auditors have no responsibility to the acquiror. The investigating accountants sign it to acknowledge that and to agree to keep any information contained therein confidential. The acquiror, however, signs it to indemnify the auditors against any action against them which might arise out of them allowing the investigating accountants access to their working papers.

This is a wide-ranging indemnity which should be read carefully and certain acquirors, particularly venture capitalists, are reluctant to give it. Sometimes minor modifications can be negotiated, although these rarely affect the scope of the indemnity. In other instances auditors will add clauses to the letter to create their own in-house standard letter which is non-negotiable.

Although the idea of giving the auditors an indemnity may be unattractive to an acquiror, in practice there is little choice if access to audit papers is to be gained. Such letters have been in common usage for a number of years and I am not aware of a claim being made against an acquiror under the indemnity clause.

INFORMATION REQUEST LISTS

In order to improve the efficiency of an investigation it is sensible to provide the target with an information request list in advance of commencing work on site. This gives the target the opportunity to prepare the principal information that the investigating accountants will require and saves time when they arrive at the target's premises. The list primarily deals with financial data and documents related to gaining an understanding of the target's financial performance.

A far more comprehensive information request list will be submitted to the vendors by the acquiror's lawyers. This list will request comprehensive details of company constitution documents, financial statements, employment contracts, sales and supply contracts, insurances, banking documents, property title deeds and leases, hire purchase agreements, rental agreements, tax documents, agency and distribution agreements, pensions documentation, etc. A combined information request list can be issued, although this can delay receipt of information that the investigating accountants require urgently. The investigating accountants should in any event ensure that there is no unnecessary duplication between the two lists. An example of a fairly comprehensive information request list is set out in Fig. 4.2.

Fig. 4.2 Information request list

1	**HISTORY AND COMMERCIAL ACTIVITIES**
1.1	Copies of audited accounts for the last three years.
1.2	Copy of the latest management accounts.
1.3	Brief account of history, location and nature of business.
1.4	Reports on the Group or its products produced by the Group or a third party.
1.5	Recent industry or product surveys.
1.6	Product catalogues and price lists.
1.7	Brief description of the production methods and techniques and the relative position of the business in relation to the 'leading edge' in the industry in which it operates.
1.8	Licensing or distribution agreements.
1.9	Details of the latest order book (with comparative figures).
1.10	Copies of agreements with major customers.
1.11	Names of any selling agents and summary of goods sold by them. Copies of agency agreements.
1.12	Copies of contracts with suppliers.
1.13	Details of alternative arrangements for important materials which are currently single sourced.
1.14	Details of subcontractors and copies of any agreements with them.
1.15	Name of suppliers who sell under Romalpa clauses (ROT).
1.16	Details of disputes with customers or suppliers.
1.17	Details of all patents, trademarks and copyrights granted or applied for showing countries covered.
1.18	Sight of minute books, and of the Memorandum and Articles of Association.
1.19	Copy of any business plans in existence.
1.20	Copy of shareholders' agreements.
1.21	Information on market and competitors.

1.22   Copies of all contracts relating to the acquisition or disposal of companies or businesses during the last six years.

1.23   Details of the current capital expenditure budget.

2   ORGANISATIONAL STRUCTURE AND EMPLOYEES

2.1   Details of management structure and division of responsibilities.

2.2   Details of all staff, including directors, providing age, length of service, salary, benefits, notice period, department and location.

2.3   List of directors and senior executives and particulars as to:

- previous experience before joining business;

- qualifications and degrees;

- duties throughout the period under review;

- age;

- years of service and date of appointment to the Board (if applicable);

- current remuneration;

- service agreements;

- pension arrangements;

- other benefits (e.g. use of company car);

- directorships of companies that carry on business of any kind with the company or its subsidiaries.

2.4   List of former directors and senior executives who have left during the period under review, with brief details.

2.5   Details of pension or retirement benefits, including a copy of the trust deed and rules, the latest scheme accounts, list of members and actuarial reports.

2.6   Copy of any union agreements and list of staff in each trade union.

2.7   Brief outline of salary/wage payment structure.

3   ACCOUNTING POLICIES AND INFORMATION SYSTEMS

3.1   Copies of accounting manuals.

3.2   Copies of last two years' auditors' management letters.

3.3   List of year end journals and reconciliation between management and statutory accounts.

3.4   Copies of consultancy reports on internal systems and controls, or Year 2000.

3.5   Copies of lease and maintenance agreements.

4   TRADING RESULTS

4.1   Analysis of turnover by main product groups for last three years.

4.2   Analysis of turnover by main customers and geographical markets for last three years.

4.3   Monthly totals of sales for the current year and previous two years.

4.4   Monthly gross profit percentage for current year and previous two years.

4.5   Analysis of purchases from principal suppliers for last three years.

5   NET ASSETS

5.1   Details of premises used by the Group, giving terms of ownership, location, size, description, dilapidation clauses, rent and rates payable and any recent valuations carried out.

5.2   Sight of any recent independent or internal valuations or insurance reports.

5.3   Copies of leases.

5.4   Copies of any dilapidation schedules served and presented by landlords.

5.5   Details of past payments of rent and rates with a summary of amounts outstanding or prepaid.

5.6   Details of all leases and tenancies granted by the Group, details of tenants and terms and assignment of leases where a Group company was the original lessee.

5.7 Comments on availability of any spare land.

5.8 Details of any premises not currently in use.

5.9 Details of all investments in other companies.

5.10 General description including age, categorised by type, of plant and machinery (or copy of fixed asset register).

5.11 List of all motor vehicles owned, leased or hired and users' names.

5.12 Details of hire purchase, lease and rental agreements.

5.13 Most recent aged listing of trade debtors.

5.14 Summary of current bad debt provisions.

5.15 Particulars of basis of valuation of stocks at each year end.

5.16 Schedule of loans made giving details of borrower, authority for loan, amount due, security, interest and repayment terms.

5.17 Most recent aged list of trade creditors.

5.18 Details of all borrowing facilities including security or guarantees given.

5.19 Any financial guarantees or indemnities given to secure credit to third parties.

5.20 Details of charges over assets of the Group.

5.21 Copies of all loan agreements.

5.22 Loan capital details: amount, repayment or conversion terms, interest rates, covenants and copies of trust deeds.

5.23 Capital commitments.

5.24 Contingent liabilities.

6   CASH FLOWS

6.1 A summary of the month end bank and cash book position for the current year and previous two years.

6.2 Copies of the latest bank reconciliations with supporting bank statements.

6.3 An explanation of the major variations in the net cash position over the last three years.

6.4   An explanation of intra-month variation in the net cash position.

7   TAXATION

7.1   Copy of the tax computations and correspondence, covering the last six years.

7.2   Copy of any apportionment clearances which have been obtained.

7.3   Copy of VAT returns for the current year and previous year.

7.4   Details of all matters outstanding with, or disputed by, the Inland Revenue.

7.5   Details of the latest control visits by PAYE, Department of Social Security (DSS) and VAT authorities and the outcome.

7.6   Copies of the latest P11Ds.

7.7   Details of any taxation or stamp duty schemes.

8   FINANCIAL PROJECTIONS

8.1   Copy of the current year's budget and estimate of trading results for current year.

8.2   Copies of profit and loss and cash flow projections together with underlying assumptions.

8.3   Details of any medium-term plans.

9   OTHER MATTERS

9.1   Copy of pension scheme documentation.

9.2   Summary of all insurance policies.

9.3   Details of any litigation, actual, threatened or pending.

PROGRESS REPORTS

Progress reports, either oral or written, should be requested at intervals throughout the duration of the investigation. In particular, matters which may be 'deal-breakers' should be raised as soon as the investigating accountants become

aware of them. It is a good discipline to set dates at weekly intervals throughout the due diligence period at which brief progress reports will be made and circulated to the advisory team.

CONFIRMATION OF ACCURACY

When a draft due diligence report is ready, many acquirors decide that they would like the target's senior management to review the draft report and confirm in writing, prior to the issue of the final report, that it is factually accurate. Where the investigation relates to a merger or a reverse takeover this confirmation may be extended to include a statement that the report does not omit any material matters relevant to the acquiror. An example of an appropriate letter is set out in Fig. 4.3.

Fig. 4.3   **Example of a confirmation of accuracy letter**

(To be typed on notepaper of company)

FAO: Senior Partner

Investigating Accountant

Address

Dear Sirs

Report on the financial affairs of XX Company Limited and Subsidiaries

With reference to the draft of the above report dated dd/mm/yy, we confirm that, to the best of our knowledge and belief, so far as the factual content is concerned, it is complete and accurate in the areas it addresses and no material matters have been omitted.

Yours faithfully

The acquiror may not wish to show the draft report to the target if it discloses matters which the acquiror intends to use in pricing or contract negotiations. It may be appropriate, therefore, to disclose selected parts of the report, but not disclose the summary of findings and those paragraphs dealing with negotiating points.

REVIEW OF PURCHASE CONTRACT

It is customary for the investigating accountant's role to continue beyond the issue of the financial due diligence report and, in particular, to use the acquired knowledge concerning the target to comment on aspects of the purchase contract. These aspects are typically as follows:

- the need for a retention of part of the consideration for a period of time and the amount of any retention;
- the warranties relating to financial information;
- the tax indemnity deed;
- the need for completion accounts to determine the target's net asset value at the completion date;
- the detailed provisions relating to the preparation of any completion accounts and, where applicable, the certification of net asset value.

In addition it is prudent to instruct the investigating accountant to review the 'disclosure letter' issued by the vendors in respect of the warranties that they are being asked to give.

5

History and commercial activities

As previously stated, the history and commercial activities of the target may be an area which some acquirors exclude from the scope of the investigation report, either because they have a good understanding of this already or because specialist commercial consultants will be reporting on it in depth. In many instances, however, this section of a report provides vital context to the reader before reaching the detailed commentary on financial matters. This is particularly the case when the report is going to senior managers/directors who are not closely involved in the acquisition, or to bankers.

Even in instances where no reference is to be made to the history and commercial activities of the target in the report, it is essential that the investigating accountants discuss history, strategy, sales and marketing, production and purchasing with management prior to reviewing financial data in detail. That review will be far more meaningful if a general understanding of the dynamics of the target and its marketplace are obtained. Most of this will be covered in the first meeting with the target's senior management.

This is an area where costs can be wasted by producing too detailed a report. While accepting, therefore, the benefits of the investigating accountants spending time on this subject, an acquiror should be specific about the level of detail to be included in the report.

Good questioning in this area, combined with some background research into markets and competitors, can often identify both commercial strengths and weaknesses. Examples of the types of issues that have arisen in the past from reviewing this area are as follows:

- the extent to which obtaining overseas sales orders is dependent upon the payment of 'commissions', sometimes in cash;

- the competitive threat of a major overseas company intending to enter the UK market;

- dependence upon one or two major customers or contracts;

- break clauses in major contracts or distribution agreements on change of ownership;

- non-arm's-length trading with parties related to the vendors;

- disputes with overseas distributors;

- forward purchase commitments running at a level in excess of current sales levels;

- the importance of the vendor's personal relationships with customers and suppliers;

- exposures to trading in a range of foreign currencies;

- recent quality control issues with subcontractors;

- a reduction in research and development (R&D) spend that is unsustainable in the future;

- changes in marketing strategy and spend impacting on the profit/loss (P/L) charge.

KEY QUESTIONS

Figure 5.1 sets out the key questions that should be asked during a review of history and commercial activities.

Fig. 5.1 Key questions to be answered

History

Are there any key turning points in the history of the business?

Are there any uncertainties over ownership of the business?

Is the capital structure unusual?

Do certain classes of equity have unusual rights or restrictions attaching to them?

Are any group companies not wholly owned?

Has the business entered into any joint ventures (JVs) or strategic alliances?

Strategy

Does the Board have a documented strategy?

Are all of the senior management team involved in setting the strategy?

Has that strategy been updated regularly?

Has the strategy changed recently?

Have external consultants advised on strategy?

Is the business planning for growth?

Markets and competitors

Are existing markets expanding, mature or contracting?

Are there new markets to attack?

Are markets particularly price sensitive?

Do management display good knowledge of their markets?

What are the major factors affecting markets?

Do any competitors dominate the market?

Are any competitors in financial difficulty?

Do competitors dictate sales prices?

Do any competitors have a technological lead?

Are any competitors winning market share?

What factors give competitors an edge over us?

Is it easy for new competitors to enter the target's market?

Are there R&D plans which will improve the target's competitive position or take us into new markets?

Is the market dependent upon or vulnerable to the general economic cycle?

Sales and marketing

Is there heavy dependence on one or several customers?

Is there any evidence of customer dissatisfaction?

Have any significant customers been lost/won recently?

Is there a documented marketing strategy?

Has advertising/sales promotion spend or direction changed recently?

Are there agency/distribution agreements?

How is the sales force motivated/reworked?

What is the impact of exchange rate movements on pricing?

Is discounting a regular trading feature?

What problems are caused by seasonality of sales?

Have returns, guarantee or warranty claims increased recently?

Are special terms given to any customers?

Are there any major or long-term sales contracts?

Are any sales made on a non-arm's-length basis?

Production

Have any production problems arisen recently?

What are the constraints on production capacity?

Is a major overhaul of production facilities required?

If so, can this be funded out of existing resources?

Are subcontracting arrangements well established?

Are alternative subcontractors available?

Are there any disputes with subcontractors?

Have there been any changes in subcontractors recently?

Is the research and development function integrated with the production function?

Has the R&D function been successful in the past?

Does management believe it has all necessary patents, trade marks and IPR?

Purchases

Is there dependence on one or several major suppliers?

What factors affect the price of purchases and are prices generally stable?

Are there alternative sources of supply?

Are there any unusual payment terms?

Have disruptions in supply arisen recently?

Are there any contracted forward purchase commitments?

Are supply difficulties a barrier to growth?

Are any purchases made on a non-arm's-length basis?

Are volume rebate agreements in place?

Premises

Are current premises adequate for the business?

Has the business planned to meet future premise requirements?

Are the directors aware of any environmental problems?

Do recent valuations differ significantly from book value?

Regulatory

Do any regulatory requirements have an impact on the conduct of the business, e.g. government quotas or consents, health and safety, consumer credit, licensing, pricing controls, minimum wage.

CONTENTS OF A DUE DILIGENCE REPORT

The contents of a due diligence report will always vary with individual circumstances but Fig. 5.2 lists the type of content that might be expected following a fairly comprehensive review.

Fig. 5.2 Matters to be included in the financial due diligence report

History:

- origin of the business;
- changes in ownership, location and activities;
- key events in past;
- current principal activities and sales/profit before tax levels;
- group structure and shareholdings.

Strategy:

- an overview of the Board's strategy.

Markets and competitors:

■ sales analysis by product service (group) and geographically;

■ market statistics, share, positioning characteristics, and growth prospects;

■ management's views thereon;

■ principal competitors and barriers to entry;

■ proposed new products/services, and R&D plans;

■ threats and opportunities.

Sales and marketing:

■ customer-base characteristics and profile;

■ major customers in recent years;

■ marketing strategy;

■ advertising and sales promotion methods;

■ overview of sales organisation;

■ distribution channels;

■ pricing policy;

■ standard sales, payment, guarantee and warranty terms

■ major contracts;

■ patterns of seasonality;

■ exposure to currency fluctuations.

Production:

■ overview of the manufacturing process, including lead times and quality control;

■ factory capacity and growth issues;

■ stockholding policy;

■ impact of new technologies;

■ current status of planned capital expenditure (CAPEX) requirements;

■ subcontracting arrangements;

■ research and development activities;

■ patents, trade marks and intellectual property rights (IPR).

Purchases:

■ principal raw materials, origin and major suppliers;

■ terms of trade, pricing volatility, payment terms, standard contracts, lead times, returns conditions and foreign exchange exposure;

■ relationships with suppliers and any material disputes;

■ quality control procedures;

■ warehousing arrangements;

■ constraints on growth.

Premises:

- existing leasehold and freehold premises;
- planned disposals or redevelopments;
- organisation needs to meet growth plans;
- recent valuations;
- planning, environmental, dilapidation issues.

Regulatory:

- impact of any regulations on the conduct of the business.

CASE STUDIES

Case study 5.1

Arrangements with suppliers

The target company was a distributor of domestic appliances in the UK, with sales of £40 million and profit before tax (PBT) of £1.5 million. During the initial discussions on the nature of the business, it was noted that volume rebates were given to the distributor by several of its largest suppliers. The company's year end was September and the volume rebates were based upon sales levels for the calendar year. No rebate was paid unless a specified annual target was achieved. Rebates were usually determined and settled by the end of February in the year following that to which the rebate related.

This appeared to be an aspect of the business that could have a significant impact on profits so the management accounts were obtained to see how rebates were treated throughout the year. Management accounts for the prior year showed rebates received of £600 000. Management accounts for the current year to June showed no rebates had been recognised. This suggested that this aspect of the business had been accounted for on a prudent basis.

However, the gross profit percentage on goods purchased from those suppliers who gave volume rebates was consistent in the current and prior years. Why should this be so if the prior year had the benefit of significant volume rebates?

When pressed on this point, management admitted that although the line of the current management accounts that related to volume rebates was 'zero', rebates had been accounted for as a reduction in cost of sales. An assumed level of rebate of £500 000 in the year to date had been processed as debit notes hidden on the purchase ledger, thus artificially reducing creditors and increasing profits.

Budgets for the rest of the year were reviewed and it became apparent that necessary targets to achieve all volume rebates would not be reached. Profits in the June management accounts were materially overstated, and the acquiror was able to renegotiate price and fully appreciate the vulnerability of the business to not achieving volume rebate targets.

Case study 5.2

CAPEX and production

During a factory tour given by the operations director to a member of the investigating accountants' team, it emerged that a major item of equipment used in a dyeing and weaving process was not on the fixed asset register. Discussion with the operations director revealed that the equipment (cost *circa* £400 000) was provided free of charge by the supplier, provided the target company bought specified quantities of chemicals every year. The target had not had any problems meeting these volumes. However, the acquiror had intended to switch to an alternative supplier for the chemicals, using its existing supply lines. Operational management had to evaluate post-acquisition the relative merits of switching supply and funding the cost of new equipment or maintaining the *status quo*.

Case study 5.3

Regulatory

A review of a tour operator revealed that the Civil Aviation Authority had recently increased its bonding requirements due to various uncertainties over the said tour operator's trading levels. The tour operator had not revealed this to the intending purchaser in the pre-heads of terms discussions and consequently the acquiror had to reconsider the implications for the forecast cash flows of the business.

6

Organisational structure and employees

The objective of including an organisational structure and employees section within a financial due diligence review is to gain an understanding of these matters and to be able to assess their impact on past and future profitability. An acquiror will be concerned if, for example:

- historical staffing levels were unsustainably low;
- salaries are below market rates or below those paid by the acquiror;
- benefit packages are inadequate;
- owner-managers have taken unrealistically low salaries;
- there is a need for significant redundancies post-completion;
- severe reductions have been made in training costs, R&D expenditure, or support services that will have to be increased in the future;
- the senior management team needs supplementing or upgrading, e.g. by the recruitment of a finance director for the first time.

All of the above will have a direct impact on the acquiror's view of the maintainable profit of the target. It will be possible to calculate an adjustment to historical profits for each item and to adjust financial projections to reflect additional costs required after a change in ownership. This may then lead to a reassessment of the value of the business.

Other issues may be identified which, although they may not be capable of translation into a figure by which historical or projected profits can be adjusted, nevertheless raise material concerns over the level of future profits. These tend to be issues such as:

- key skill shortages;
- high staff turnover;
- the recent loss of key employees, particularly good salespeople;
- low staff morale;
- a management style which conflicts with that of the acquiror.

These are all issues which can affect the sustainability of current profits and constrain growth. Even if they are excluded from the investigating accountant's remit, they are all matters that management will need to consider.

44

KEY QUESTIONS

Figure 6.1 sets out the key questions that should be asked during a review of organisational structure and employees.

Fig. 6.1 Key questions to be answered

Has the business got a documented organisation chart? If not, why not?

Does the organisation chart show gaps or imbalances in responsibility?

Is there a balanced management team?

Is one individual dominant in the business?

Are there clear weaknesses in the team?

Does the management team meet regularly to review business performance and are these meetings minuted?

Do proposed senior recruits appear to be suitably experienced/qualified?

Are the terms of senior managers' employment appropriate?

Are any payments made to senior managers' wives, related parties or related companies?

Has the business been damaged by the recent loss of key people?

Has management succession been planned?

Are employee remuneration/benefit packages competitive?

Is there a wage review imminent and, if so, what is the expected overall increase?

Are salary/wage rates and total benefit packages in line with those of the acquiror?

Are the growth prospects of the business threatened by skill shortages?

Have staff turnover rates increased, or are they particularly high?

Is training spend adequate?

What is the industrial relations record of the business?

Are there any planned redundancies or wrongful dismissal claims?

What does the business need to do to comply with Cadbury Code of Best Practice and Greenbury Committee recommendations?

CONTENTS OF A DUE DILIGENCE REPORT

The contents of a due diligence report will always vary with individual circumstances but Fig. 6.2 lists the type of content that might be expected following a fairly comprehensive review.

Fig. 6.2 Matters to be included in the financial due diligence report

- Organisation chart.

- Overview of the management structure, culture and style.

- Details of agenda and frequency of various management meetings.

- Details of senior executives and key personnel, including experience, duties, qualifications, shareholdings, age, years of service, service contracts, remuneration, benefits, pensions, incentive schemes, loans, payments to wives or connected parties/companies.

- Policy adopted to training/recruiting successors.

- Changes in senior management in the period under review.

- Strengths and weaknesses of the management team.

- Proposed additions to the senior management team.

- Proposed compensation for loss of office.

- Analyse the employee profile by appropriate categories (location, function, full/part time, etc.).

- Overview of recruitment, training and development policies and practices.

- Staff turnover and special skill requirements/shortages.

- Salary and wage structure, including basic pay, overtime, bonuses, holidays, welfare services, benefits, pensions, PRP, share option schemes, loans, government job grants.

- Date of next/last pay review.

- Union representation and state of industrial relations.

- Compliance with the Cadbury Code of Best Practice.

- Compliance with the recommendations of the Greenbury Committee.

CASE STUDIES

Case study 6.1

Dependence on key people skills

The target was a developer of computer games which had grown rapidly during the previous 18 months as a result of two 'hit' games that were each developing into a series of 'next generation' games.

Although the key games development personnel were included in the employee list and noted therein as being among the company's highest paid employees, they were actually self-employed consultants. This came to light when copies of employment contracts were requested.

Further enquiry revealed that the agreements between the company and the key consultants had been drafted by the vendor without legal advice. The agreements had no notice period for termination, were not entirely clear on the basis upon which royalty payments were due, and raised a significant doubt as to who owned the intellectual property rights to the games developed by the consultants.

When the consultants were offered new agreements that attempted to clarify the above points and retrospectively protect the company's IPR, several refused to sign. The transaction was consequently aborted.

Case study 6.2

Benefits

Certain employees at a target company in the leisure industry were found to have been provided with accommodation free of charge.

There was considered to be an additional liability to PAYE as the 'benefit' had not been returned on the individuals' P11Ds and the individuals did not fall within Inland Revenue exemptions where accommodation can be provided, without being assessable, providing various conditions are met (proper performance of duties, etc.).

The acquirer obtained protection from any past liabilities by obtaining a specific indemnity from the vendors.

7

Accounting policies and information systems

ACCOUNTING POLICIES

This area is fundamental to financial due diligence, even in situations where the overall scope of the due diligence has been minimised. Reported profits can vary materially depending upon the accounting policies and practices adopted by the reporting entity. Aggressive accounting policies can materially increase reported profits and lead to acquirors paying far too much for a business. Two examples of the impact of a particular accounting policy on reported profits are set out in Figs 7.1 and 7.2.

Fig. 7.1 Maintenance contract income recognition

Company A (the target) sells business telephone systems and associated maintenance contracts. In the final month of its accounting period annual maintenance contracts with a value of £600 000 were invoiced. The contracts cover the 12 months ahead, are non-cancellable and in most instances full payment is received within one month of invoicing. A gross margin of 90 per cent is made on maintenance contracts.

Company A, with the agreement of its auditors, recognised the full £600 000 of income in its accounts in the month in which it was invoiced and established a provision of 10 per cent of the invoiced amount to cover the future cost of servicing the contracts. £540 000 of profit was consequently included in the accounting period just ending, in respect of those maintenance contracts.

Company B (the acquiror) also sells telephone system maintenance contracts, but instead of recognising all income in the month of invoicing it recognises the income, and the associated costs, evenly over the period to which the contract relates.

If Company B's more prudent accounting policy is applied to Company A, £50 000 of income and £45 000 of profit would have been included in the accounting period just ended.

From Company B's perspective, Company A's reported profits, upon which it based its offer to buy the company, were overstated by £495 000 in respect of the final month accounting. This figure would be reduced by an equivalent adjustment to the previous year's accounts, but the net effect would still have been a material overstatement of profits.

Fig. 7.2 Amortisation of exhibition costs

A specialised engineering company attends its key industry trade fair every two years. Customers from around the world attend the trade fair, which is held in different locations in Europe, North America and Asia. The cost of the stand, staffing the trade fair, entertaining clients, shipping equipment out, marketing, insurance, travel, publicity, associated advertising, etc. was £240 000.

The trade fair took place in the last quarter of the recently ended accounting period ('Year 1'). Some of the accounting policies that could be adopted, and the impact that each would have on reported profits, are as follows:

	Charge against profits		
	Year 1 £000	Year 2 £000	Year 3 £000
1 Recognise costs fully in the year in which costs were incurred	(240)	—	—
2 Spread costs over next 12 months as management believes that the company benefits from sales orders over that period	(60)	(180)	—
3 Spread costs over the 24 months until the next trade fair but recognising more costs in earlier periods as that is when greatest benefit arises, say	(80)	(120)	(40)
4 As above, but spread costs evenly	(30)	(120)	(90)

There are many areas where a particular transaction can be accounted for in a number of different ways, each of which can be justified in certain circumstances to an auditor. Although the statutory accounts of a company contain a statement of its accounting policies, the wording of those policies is often very general. It is vital to an appreciation of profitability that an acquiror looks beneath the stated policies and gains a thorough understanding of the underlying methods used to implement those policies.

INFORMATION SYSTEMS

Whatever its accounting policies and practices, a company's systems will determine its ability to report its trading results accurately. An assessment of systems is vital in appraising the reliability of reported profitability and the carrying value of assets and liabilities.

Information systems are also important in supporting views upon how well managed and controlled the business appears to be. Effective systems, together with a timely monthly management information package, are a good indication that the business is tightly managed against planned performance. A cavalier approach towards internal monthly reporting inevitably results in the financial due diligence process needing to be extended in both scope and duration. If a company has been groomed for sale over a period of time and its systems are still weak and uninformative, then an acquiror needs to be very wary.

KEY QUESTIONS

Figure 7.3 sets out the key questions that should be asked during a review of accounting policy and systems.

Fig. 7.3 Key questions to be answered

Are all key accounting policies disclosed in the Annual Financial Statements?

Are the policies acceptable and consistent with industry norms?

Are all of the practices adopted to implement those policies acceptable?

Are all the policies/practices consistent with those of the acquiror?

What will be the impact of changing accounting policies to those of the acquiror?

Have reported profits been affected by changes in accounting policies?

Are the management information systems fully integrated?

Is the business dependent on third parties for software/hardware maintenance?

Are systems security measures adequate?

Has the business reviewed whether its systems are millennium compliant?

Have systems weaknesses been noted in auditors' management letters?

Do information technology (IT) consultants need to carry out a detailed review?

Are the management information systems producing timely and reliable information?

What key performance indicators does the business use to monitor its performance?

Are there systems to ensure effective cash management?

Are the month end accounting procedures relating to depreciation, stock, provisions, accounts and income recognition reasonable?

Are there many adjustments made to year end management accounts to produce Annual Financial Statements?

Is the quality/quantity of information contained in the monthly management accounts pack adequate?

Are variances from budget explained?

Does the budgetary process involve appropriate input from non-financial personnel?

Are regular budgets produced, are variances monitored and are budgets updated during the year?

Are medium-term plans prepared?

CONTENTS OF A DUE DILIGENCE REPORT

The contents of a due diligence report will always vary with individual circumstances but Fig. 7.4 lists the type of content that might be expected following a fairly comprehensive review.

Fig. 7.4 Matters to be included in the financial due diligence report

- Summary of the key accounting policies and practices.

- Explanation of unacceptable/contentious accounting policies/practices.

- Changes in accounting policies in the period under review.

- Amendments required by anticipated changes in UK generally accepted accounting principles (GAAP).

- Differences between policies of the business and the acquiror.

- Differences between policies and industry norms.

- Overview description of the management information systems.

- Management's views on adequacy, capacity and future development of systems.

- Ownership and maintenance of software.

- Third party maintenance contracts.

- Backup facilities.

- Extent of management's consideration of millennium compliance and impact of the Euro.

- Nature of monthly management information systems output.

- Cash management systems.

- Overview of the internal control environment.

- Significant weaknesses in management information systems.

- Overview of the budgetary and planning procedures.

- Deficiencies in the quality/adequacy of previous audit work.

CASE STUDIES

Case study 7.1

Stock valuation accounting policy

The target was an advanced instrumentation company manufacturing high value items to exacting specifications. Summary financial information was as follows:

	£m	Prior year £m
Sales	10.0	7.8
Gross profit	4.0	2.6
Profit before tax	2.0	1.0
Profit after tax	1.4	0.7
Net assets	2.5	

This was an attractive niche business with good technology and strong growth in profits. Based upon a price/earnings (P/E) ratio of 10, a price of £14 million was agreed with the vendors.

Gross profit percentage had increased from 33 per cent to 40 per cent in the last accounting period and the due diligence work naturally sought to explain the reasons for this.

The accounting policy for stock valuation was reviewed and appeared to be satisfactory. Manufactured items were valued at the cost of raw materials, components and production labour. The latter was costed at £18 per hour and this was reasonable in light of salary levels and annual productive hours. There was some evidence of pricing increases, but not enough to justify a 7 per cent margin improvement.

Management was asked if the stock accounting policy had been changed, and stated that it had not. A detailed review of the previous year's audit files, however, revealed that while the policy had not been changed, the value at which production labour was included in stock had previously been £8 per hour. An artificially low stock valuation in the previous year had reduced reported profits and the tax payable thereon.

The prior year stock under valuation was effectively released to profit in the current year, overstating the profit in the current year by £0.3 million. Profits after tax were therefore overstated by some £0.2 million resulting in the consideration of £14 million being inflated by £2 million.

Case study 7.2
Upgrade of information systems

The target was a distributor of office equipment selling direct to major companies operating from many locations and to hundreds of independent office equipment retailers throughout the UK. Profits before tax for the last calendar year were just under £1 million, although current year management accounts indicated a significantly lower level of profitability. The acquiror, who was a direct competitor of the target, had agreed a price of £4 million based upon a belief that significant cost savings could be made by rationalising the warehousing and distribution operations of both companies. The vendor was applying pressure to complete the deal very quickly with the common threat of another interested buyer being used to pressurise the acquiror.

The target had recently invested in a new integrated stock, distribution and invoicing system. The acquiror had excellent systems of its own and no plans to use the new systems post completion. It therefore restricted the systems due diligence work to a brief overview.

However, the general accounting control environment was poor, the finance director did not have a good understanding of the new systems and IT consultants' fees were still being incurred on a monthly basis. Consequently the scope of systems due diligence was amended.

A more detailed review revealed that the new system had been giving a full sales discount on the total value of orders when only a part-delivery was made. When the balance of the order was dispatched, a further sales discount would be given. It had taken the target three months to realise that this was happening and attempts were then made to re-invoice customers for £300 000 of discounts given in error. Many customers were refusing to pay, extensive bad will was generated throughout the client base leading to reductions in new orders, and assets and profits were overstated.

Concern over the damage to customer relations was one of the major factors that led to this deal being aborted.

Trading results

The investigating accountants should use, in the review of trading results, all of the knowledge of the company's operations, accounting policies and information systems that they have acquired in their review to date. In this way, the acquiror's main questions can be dealt with, namely:

- are the profit figures upon which the price has been based stated on a reasonable basis;

- are there any exceptional items that could affect the acquiror's view on price;

- what are the principal features and characteristics of the recent trading results and trends?

In order to answer these questions, and the many ancillary questions that spring from them, the investigating accountants will review significant amounts of data, often relating to the previous three years. That data might include statutory accounts, monthly management accounts, budgets, sales analyses and reports, sales order analyses, time records, contract accounting summaries, deferred income schedules, overhead analyses, costing information, board minutes, customer correspondence files and many other sources of information. For groups of companies, or those which operate on a divisional basis, separate trading reviews may be necessary for each part of the business, with a group overview section pulling together the key points.

Trading results can be reviewed in great detail, with minor variances from budget or year-on-year movements each being explained for individual categories of sales and costs. The cost of doing this, however, needs to be weighed against the benefits to be gained from such a detailed process. Acquirors entering a new market or overseas territory tend to request very detailed trading reviews, using this part of the process to build up their general knowledge of the target's operations. Most acquirors, however, set a reasonable materiality level and seek more information on sales and gross margins than on overhead costs.

A three-year trading review frequently identifies exceptional and non-recurring income or cost items that need to be brought to an acquiror's attention. This should be done in a clear and prominent manner, preferably in the form of a table near the beginning of the trading review section of the financial due diligence report.

KEY QUESTIONS

Figure 8.1 sets out the key questions that should be asked during a review of trading results.

Fig. 8.1 Key questions to be answered

What are the key features of the overall trend of trading results during the period under review?

Were trends in line with expectations?

Can significant variances from budget be explained?

Is there a seasonal pattern to sales?

Has the sales mix changed and, if so, why?

Have major customers been won/lost?

Are there any exceptional/non-recurring revenues?

Have unit prices increased or come under severe pressure?

What has been the impact of new markets/products?

Is there dependence upon large contracts or sales to related parties?

Are rebates or discounts given/received and, if so, has the basis of calculation changed in the period under review?

Why have gross profit percentages changed?

Have the elements of cost of sales changed?

Have changes in suppliers affected margins?

Have commodity price or exchange rate movements affected margins?

Does the business commit to buy forward from suppliers?

Are goods or services purchased from related parties?

Is the performance of the business consistent with its industry peers?

Have margins been affected by exceptional sales deals or one-off costs of sale?

Has deferred/accrued income been appropriately and consistently recognised?

Can significant increases/decreases in individual overhead expense categories be explained?

Are there any exceptional/non-recurring costs?

Are there any costs borne outside the target business or assets used by the business at a non-arm's-length cost?

Have excess directors/related party costs been incurred?

Is the overall trend of overhead costs consistent with the pattern of growth of the business?

Are there material costs that clearly will not be incurred under the new ownership?

Are there any material additional costs that will be incurred under the new ownership?

Is the basis of allocation of costs between different subsidiaries, activities or divisions reasonable?

Is the finance income/cost consistent with the cash/borrowing position of the business?

What is the impact on recent profitability of provisions being created or released?

Is the underlying profitability of the business materially different from reported profitability?

CONTENTS OF A DUE DILIGENCE REPORT

The contents of a due diligence report will always vary with individual circumstances but Fig. 8.2 lists the type of content that might be expected following a fairly comprehensive review.

Fig. 8.2   **Matters to be included in the financial due diligence report**

- Summary of the last three years' trading results.

- Explanation of source or basis of preparation of figures.

- Analysis of sales by region, location, product group, service type, as appropriate.

- Appropriate analysis of cost of sales and gross margins.

- Explanation of key trends in sales and gross margins.

- Explanation of gross profit trend.

- Analysis of overheads.

- Explanation of significant changes in overhead costs.

- Explanation of the nature of certain costs.

- Comparisons with budgets.

- Reasons for variances from budgets.

- Exceptional/non-recurring items affecting profits.

- Analysis of finance costs.

- Operating costs borne by other group/related companies.

- Adjusted underlying profitability of the target.

- Related party transactions.

- Comparisons of performance and key ratios against industry norms/benchmarks.

CASE STUDIES

Accelerated depreciation

The target was a software development company that had a strong growth record. Sales and costs had increased significantly during the last three completed accounting periods, but depreciation costs had increased at a particularly high rate.

The reason for this was that some 18 months previously it had been decided to halve the depreciation period for computer equipment and fixtures and fittings from four years and ten years to two years and five years respectively. This prudent accounting policy had reduced reported profits to a lower level than would have been reported if the acquiror's accounting policies had been applied. The acquiror, therefore, was comforted by this analysis.

Further analysis connected to the review of the current incomplete accounting period, however, changed the acquiror's view. The agreed price was based upon a multiple of current year profits. Those profits were stated after a significantly reduced depreciation charge as most of the target's computer equipment was fully depreciated. That equipment would, however, need to be replaced within the next 12 months and an annual depreciation charge would again be levied against the profit and loss account.

The effect of the target's prudent accounting policy, therefore, was a one-off increase to profits in the year of sale, resulting in too high a price having been agreed.

Estimates in management accounts

There are a large number of companies in the UK that do not produce good monthly packages of financial information. Frequently incurred problems include producing figures quarterly rather than monthly, not including comparisons with budget and prior year, not explaining principal features, variances and fluctuations, and taking a broad approach to producing information by including estimates for certain key figures.

An example of the latter is a target engineering group with operations in six different locations, each of which had a different accounting system and reporting format, but all of which used an estimate of cost of sales and monthly stock in their management accounts. In fact, it was assumed that stock levels were constant throughout the year and that the opening stock figure did not move.

The group was profitable and cash generative, and the vendors felt that the management accounts were accurate enough for their purposes. The acquiror, however, requested an interim stocktake to gain additional assurance on current profit levels. Predictably, this revealed a significantly lower stock figure, thus demonstrating that the management accounts understated cost of sales and overstated profits.

Case study 8.3

Group charges

It is common in groups of companies for certain categories of cost to be incurred centrally and to be re-charged out to subsidiaries or divisions. Such costs might include audit costs, property rentals, group management salaries, insurances, finance costs, a central human resources department, IT costs, costs of the finance function, etc.

Vendors are often keen to point out that past group charges are excessive and bear little relation to the actual costs of providing these services in the future. They should, therefore, be treated as an add-back to reported profits, thus increasing them and leading to a higher price being supportable. Sometimes this is the case, but equally often services are provided at no cost to the business being sold.

An investigation into a diverse industrial group highlighted the care that needs to be taken in this area. Certain re-charges to the target, calculated on the basis of the percentage of group turnover that arose in the target, would definitely not be incurred in the future. Prominent among such costs were the substantial employment costs of the board of a listed PLC. However, property costs were all incurred centrally and the target was re-charged at below market rates, significant marketing and brand awareness costs were reported centrally or even in other subsidiaries, and the re-charge for pension costs had been reduced recently for reasons that would not apply if the target was an independent company.

On balance, the target would clearly incur a far higher level of costs in the future than it had reported in its profit and loss accounts in the past. This led to a price renegotiation.

Net assets

There are some businesses where the value of the target's net assets is equally or more important than its historic or current profitability. These include, for example, property, hotels, oil, leasing and plant hire businesses. For some of these businesses asset value, perhaps discounted at an appropriate industry 'norm', is the starting point when considering value. Earnings are of secondary concern.

An acquiror will normally employ valuers to advise upon the current worth of the principal assets of such businesses, whether they are property, mineral reserves, used cars or heavy tools. Such valuers will not normally comment on the other assets and liabilities in the target's balance sheet, all of which may impact on the final price paid for the business. Therefore, a line by line review of the balance sheet by the investigating accountants should still be undertaken even in such circumstances.

More typically, earnings will be the primary concern of the acquiror. The review of the balance sheet should explain the nature of the target's assets and liabilities, the basis upon which assets have been valued and liabilities recognised, and the impact that over/undervaluations have upon profitability.

Much of the detail required for this review can usually be obtained from the audit files. The extent to which the auditors have physically verified fixed assets, counted stock, checked debtor collections and tested creditor cut-off will be important in gaining a high level of comfort. For the reasons stated previously, the relevant audit files may be rather thin and it may be necessary for the investigating accountant to perform limited audit tests in certain areas. Particular attention should be paid to the inclusion of all liabilities in the balance sheet.

Acquirors sometimes purchase the trade and assets of a business rather than the company. When this happens it is still prudent to review the most recent audited balance sheet of the business in its entirety. This will help the acquiror to gauge the total capital requirement of the business going forward and to identify past balance sheet practices that may have had a distorting effect on reported profits.

KEY QUESTIONS

Figure 9.1 sets out the key questions that should be asked during a review of net assets.

Fig. 9.1 Key questions to be answered

Are intangible assets reasonably valued?

Are total asset values supported by detailed analyses/registers?

Are there any recent independent asset valuation reports?

Are depreciation rates adequate?

Are any assets undervalued?

Has any interest, own labour or materials been capitalised?

Is stock valued appropriately, particularly where overheads are included?

How is long-term work in progress (WIP) valued and profit recognised?

Have stock qualities been physically verified recently?

What levels of stock loss have arisen on recent stock counts?

How are slow-moving/obsolete stock lines identified and provided for?

Have stock levels increased or decreased?

Are stocks held by third parties fairly valued?

Is the ageing of trade debtors improving or deteriorating, and is it acceptable?

Are bad debt reserves created on a reasonable basis?

What is the past experience of bad debts?

Is the business vulnerable to one or two large debtors defaulting?

Are normal credit terms being enforced with all customers?

Are there any unusual sundry debtors or prepayments?

Is accrued income appropriately calculated?

Is the level of cash at the balance sheet date representative of the cash held throughout the month/year?

What are the overdraft facilities?

How is surplus cash managed?

Who are the principal creditors?

Does the business receive any special credit terms?

Is the business under pressure to pay creditors more quickly?

Do any creditor balances attract interest or offer discounts for early payment?

What are the terms of bank loans/overdrafts?

Are there any unusual sundry creditors or accruals?

How is deferred income calculated?

Are provisions properly made and appropriately calculated?

What is the nature of any long-term liabilities, such as hire purchase (HP) and finance lease obligations?

Are there any loans from shareholders or connected parties that could be repayable in the short term?

Are there any unusual reserves or restrictions on distributions to shareholders?

CONTENTS OF A DUE DILIGENCE REPORT

The contents of a due diligence report will always vary with individual circumstances but Fig. 9.2 lists the type of content that might be expected following a fairly comprehensive review.

Fig. 9.2 Matters to be included in the financial due diligence report

- Summary of the assets and liabilities of the business for the last two years.

- Explanation of source or basis of preparation of figures.

- Analyses of individual categories of assets and liabilities.

- Explanation of the valuation bases of assets, including tangible fixed assets, stock, WIP and debtors.

- Comments on the adequacy of provisions against asset values.

- Explanation of the basis of recognition of liabilities.

- Financing facilities and terms of loans/overdrafts.

- Unrecognised or unrealised revaluation surpluses.

- Comments on the reason for major variances between current and prior balance sheets.

CASE STUDIES

Case study 9.1

Phantom assets

The target was a developer of computer-aided design programs for several niche industries. A comparison of the last two balance sheets revealed substantial expenditure in the last year on computer hardware and software. Like many companies, the target did not maintain a fixed asset register but the value of computer equipment was so significant that the investigating accountants tried to reconstruct a listing of major items.

The value of items on that list was substantially less than the total in the balance sheet and, in particular, one item of £600 000 could not be supported by purchase invoices. This item did not relate to equipment, but rather to the buy-back of product distribution rights from the ex-European distributor. The target had capitalised the cost, was depreciating it over three years and had claimed capital allowances on the expenditure. Not only were significant adjustments made to the balance sheet and reported profits, but the target's tax liability increased.

Case study 9.2

Stock over-valuation

Company X had negotiated a price to acquire Company Y, a multi-site specialist sports clothing retailer. The price was to be adjusted according to net assets shown in completion accounts. Due diligence revealed that, although stock records of quantities could be relied upon throughout the year, the appropriateness of stock valuation was questionable; rigorous application of provisions for slow-moving items or ends of ranges tended to be made only once a year before the company's annual sale and just prior to the year end. The timing of the proposed acquisition meant that stock per management records could have been overvalued, since the acquisition was timed to take place a month before the annual write-down process.

As a result, the due diligence process made specific recommendations as to the stock-provisioning formulae to be applied in the completion accounts. In addition, specific slow-moving items were identified by the reporting accountants, e.g. large numbers of size three and size twelve boots where no other sizes were still stocked in the range. These findings resulted in write-downs of £200 000 which directly impacted on the price paid.

Taxation

Taxation issues surrounding the acquisition of a business are so extensive and complex that they are the subject of many substantial books. Tax due diligence should always be undertaken by tax specialists and should be linked to the tax structuring advice given on a transaction. It is not possible, therefore, to summarise here the many substantive tax issues that need to be considered as part of the overall due diligence process.

Clearly, close co-operation between the investigating accountants' team and the tax due diligence team is essential. Frequently, but by no means always, they will be drawn from the same firm. The investigating accountants may act as an initial information gatherer for the tax specialists, and this briefing has been drafted on that basis. Consequently, the investigating accountants will concentrate on establishing the general status of the target's corporation tax, payroll tax and VAT affairs. They will ascertain how up to date those affairs are, whether there are disputes with any tax authorities, when the most recent tax inspections took place, whether any taxes are overdue, and whether the target has had an aggressive approach to tax planning.

At one end of the spectrum, after such enquiries it may be clear that the target's tax affairs are straightforward and up to date. No further work may be deemed necessary. At the other, issues such as group reconstructions, international transfer pricing and a history of disputed tax computations will require extensive tax due diligence. This is an area where no sensible acquiror takes short cuts, notwithstanding the extensive tax indemnity which is usually given by the vendor in the sale agreement.

KEY QUESTIONS

Figure 10.1 sets out the key questions that should be asked during a review of taxation.

Fig. 10.1 Key questions to be answered

Has the business experienced an abnormally high or low effective tax rate and, if so, why?

Are recent tax computations agreed by the Inland Revenue?

What issues are being disputed by the Inland Revenue?

Are any agreed tax losses restricted in their availability?

Is there a backlog of tax payable to any authority?

Has the business entered into any tax planning schemes in recent years?

Is a more detailed tax review required by tax consultancy?

When was the last PAYE inspection and what was the result?

Are there any share schemes or other tax-efficient schemes that require a detailed review?

When was the last VAT inspection and what was the result?

Are there particular VAT complications that require an expert review?

CONTENTS OF A DUE DILIGENCE REPORT

The contents of a due diligence report will always vary with individual circumstances but Fig. 10.2 lists the type of content that might be expected following a fairly comprehensive review.

Fig. 10.2 **Matters to be included in the financial due diligence report**

- Recent effective tax rate.

- Most recently agreed corporation tax computations.

- Agreed tax losses.

- Advance corporation tax (ACT) payable/recoverable.

- Disputes with the tax authorities.

- Reasons for delays in submitting/agreeing computations.

- Recent reconstructions, reorganisations and tax clearance applications.

- Date and result of last VAT inspection.

- Date and result of last PAYE/NIC inspection.

- Fines and penalties paid recently.

Cash flow

Understanding the cash generating abilities and the annual pattern of cash flow of a business is vital to a proper assessment of value. Much of the information required to do this will have been obtained already by the time this section of the review is undertaken. During the reviews of commercial activities, trading results and net assets, the investigating accountant will have learnt the following:

■ the standard credit terms offered to customers and received from suppliers;

■ special credit arrangements agreed with certain customers or suppliers;

■ arrangements for payment on account;

■ the variability of monthly sales and expenditure;

■ the extent of bad debts;

■ historical levels of capital expenditure;

■ the need for future capital expenditure;

■ average debtor days;

■ average creditor days;

■ stockholding levels and patterns;

■ changes in any of the above to reflect new business practices;

■ current backlogs in paying creditors;

■ tax, national insurance and VAT payment timings;

■ cash and overdraft levels;

■ loan finance levels and repayment requirements;

■ lease payment commitments.

A review of historical cash flows and the pattern of cash flow over the previous 12 months should confirm that the above matters have been properly understood. Major trends should be highlighted, as should exceptional cash inflows and outflows. Frequent breaches of overdraft limits or examples of additional finance being arranged at short notice are key indicators of poor cash management or unpredictable cashflows.

KEY QUESTIONS

Figure 11.1 sets out the key questions that should be asked during a review of cash flow.

Fig. 11.1 Key questions to be answered

Is the overall pattern of cash flow affected by seasonal factors?

What are the principal uses of cash generated by operations?

How has growth been funded?

Has there been significant CAPEX?

Are borrowing facilities appropriate to cash requirements?

Are there any exceptional cash inflows or outflows?

CONTENTS OF A DUE DILIGENCE REPORT

The contents of a due diligence report will always vary with individual circumstances but Fig. 11.2 lists the type of content that might be expected following a fairly comprehensive review.

Fig. 11.2 Matters to be included in the financial due diligence report

- Summary of the last three years' cash flows.

- Comments on the significant features thereof.

- Patterns and seasonality in cash flows.

- Recent breaches of borrowing facility limits and/or covenants.

- Exceptional/non-recurring cash inflows or outflows.

12

Financial projections

The key objective of most financial due diligence exercises is to assist the acquiror in forming an opinion on the target's level of maintainable profits. The most reliable indicator of maintainable profits may be recent and current profit levels, but an assessment of the current year budget, and perhaps projections for periods beyond that, is often a key part of the investigation.

Before reviewing any numbers, the previous budgeting accuracy of the target and the amount of effort put into the production of the budget should be assessed. Many small and medium-sized companies do not produce a budget or, if they do, it merely sets out sales targets and is rarely referred to during the year. Others produce a budget but neither update it during the budgeted period nor periodically consider the specific reasons for actual variances against it. At the other end of the scale, larger companies, businesses that are part of larger groups and tightly controlled smaller enterprises use their budgets to plan the future and monitor actual performance against that plan. The amount of effort put into the budgeting process and the use made of the budget as a live management tool will affect the scope of work done in this area.

Whatever is available should be reviewed in an appropriate level of detail. If no forecasts are available, the target should be asked to produce them as a special exercise and, in particular, the underlying assumptions should be carefully documented. If possible, managers who are not vendors and who are continuing in the business post-completion should be involved in the review of financial projections.

Each material assumption should be discussed with the target's management and assessed for its reasonableness. Clearly, where the continuation of current sales, margins and cost levels is assumed, then it is likely that the investigating accountant will be able to give a strong level of comfort on the projections. This, however, is rarely the situation. An expectation of current year's profits is usually given during early discussions between the target and the acquiror. That expectation is usually more than last year's profit and frequently a lot higher than last year. The assumptions being probed by the investigating accountant tend to be fairly aggressive in terms of higher sales, improved margins, and costs rising at a lower rate than sales. The review process seeks to identify factors which tangibly support the assumption (e.g. new customers, distributors or product lines) and highlight those assumptions which are currently based purely on a future intention (e.g. a future price rise or the opening of an overseas sales office later in the year).

Acquirors want to form a view on the achievability of financial projections and not unnaturally press investigating accountants to be unequivocal in their views. While no investigating accountant will be able or willing to say that a particular forecast will be achieved, some will express far more opinions than others who prefer to do no more than describe the basis of any forecast. This is an issue worth

exploring at the time of selecting investigating accountants as it can be very disappointing to read a report on financial projections which is devoid of any opinions.

Where the acquiror intends to substantially reorganise the target post-completion or merge it with its own operations, it may be more appropriate for the investigating accountants to review the acquiror's projections. Views on the achievability of certain cost savings, the potential loss of customers, the costs of closure or redundancy, and other integration issues should all be sought by the acquiror.

Whether reviewing the target's or the acquiror's projections, the impact of key sensitivities on the achievement of the projections should be reviewed and summarised. These sensitivities (e.g. the impact of a 10 per cent sales shortfall or the loss of a major contract) should be discussed and agreed with the acquiror prior to being included in the due diligence report.

KEY QUESTIONS

Figure 12.1 sets out the key questions that should be asked during a review of financial projections.

Fig. 12.1 **Key questions to be answered**

What are the key trends presented in the projections summary?

Have budgets/forecasts in the last two years been accurate?

If not, what reasons does management give for this?

Have the projections been prepared especially for our review or are they normal operating budgets?

Was the overall method of preparation sufficiently diligent and detailed?

Were operational as well as financial staff involved in their preparation?

Have the projections been approved by the Board?

Are the projections arithmetically accurate?

Do the projections assume any changes in accounting policies or bases?

Has a projected balance sheet at the end of the projected period been prepared? If not, why not?

Are projected sales levels higher than recent/current levels?

Is projected sales growth supported by long order books, new customers, new products, new distributors, or allocations against specific customers?

Is projected sales growth volume or price based?

Is projected sales growth supported by the general trading climate for that industry?

Is the rate of growth consistent with that achieved in the past?

Are there any factors such as customer/contract losses, capacity reductions or pricing pressures that suggest sales growth will be difficult?

Are projected changes in gross margins supported by current achievements, known price rises, cost reductions or firmly priced orders/contracts?

Are projected costs in line with recently experienced levels?

Are there any projected cost savings that depend upon future actions?

To what extent has the business incurred unpredictable costs in the past (e.g. material bad debts or stock write-offs, closure costs, warranty or rectification costs, contract penalties, etc.)?

Can the timing of cash inflows/outflows be forecast with reasonable confidence, or is historic experience one of unpredictability?

Are reductions being projected in stock levels or debtor days?

Are increases being projected in creditor days?

What is the revised profit and cash flow position after sensitising the projections to adjust those sales, gross profit, cost and cash flow assumptions that are not supported by currently achieved operating performance?

CONTENTS OF A DUE DILIGENCE REPORT

The contents of a due diligence report will always vary with individual circumstances but Fig. 12.2 lists the type of content that might be expected following a fairly comprehensive review.

Fig. 12.2 Matters to be included in the financial due diligence report

- Summary of the financial projections with appropriate analyses.

- Previous forecasting accuracy.

- Basis of preparation.

- Arithmetical accuracy.

- Changes in accounting policies/bases.

- Assumptions underlying the projections.

- Commentary on the reasonableness of the assumptions.

- Key sensitivities.

- Impact of key sensitivities on the projections.

Other matters

Many financial due diligence reports have a section at the end to deal with sundry matters which do not fit easily within other sections. These matters are normally requests for information and rarely involve any analysis or appraisal of the data obtained in connection with them. It is convenient for the investigating accountants to gather this information while on site and adds to the overall comprehensiveness of the more detailed type of financial due diligence report.

Having said that, it is very easy for such issues to be time-consuming and involve the production of a large volume of appendices in which various agreements are set out. There is a real risk that this will duplicate the work of the acquiror's lawyers who, in any event, will not only obtain those agreements but will review them in detail. A conversation between the investigating accountants and lawyers is needed to ensure that this does not happen.

Material issues can arise out of the matters typically covered, e.g. contingent liabilities and legal actions against the target can lead to transactions being aborted. It is fair to say, however, that the acquiror's lawyers would be expected to identify such significant matters during legal due diligence. The acquiror should not, therefore, rely upon the investigating accountant as the principal reviewer of this data.

KEY QUESTIONS

Figure 13.1 sets out the key questions that should be asked during a review of other matters.

Fig. 13.1 Key questions to be answered
Is there any material litigation in progress, threatened or planned?
How frequently has the business been involved in litigation in the past?
Are there any contingent liabilities (e.g. guarantees, warranties)?
Does the business have a summary of its insurance cover?
Has the level of insurance cover been reviewed recently?
Are there material future commitments under rental/operating lease agreements?
What pension arrangements exist for employees?
Are defined benefit schemes fully funded?
Are there any agreements with third parties (distribution, IPR, JVs, cooperation, etc.) which are significant to operations?
What capital commitments have been made?

CONTENTS OF A DUE DILIGENCE REPORT

The contents of a due diligence report will always vary with individual circumstances but Fig. 13.2 lists the type of content that might be expected following a fairly comprehensive review.

Fig. 13.2 **Matters to be included in the financial due diligence report**

- Litigation in progress or pending.

- Contingent liabilities.

- Insurances.

- Rental/lease agreements.

- Pension schemes and actuarial valuations.

- Third party agreements.

- Capital commitments.

CASE STUDY

Case study 13.1

Future pension commitments

Company X, with existing manufacturing businesses in both the UK and the Netherlands, commissioned due diligence into a business with similar operations in both countries. A review of the target's pension fund revealed that:

- the benefits in the Netherlands were not as advantageous as those provided by Company X to its own employees;

- the pension fund was regarded as underfunded in regard to part-time UK employees.

The acquiror intended to merge the operations in the Netherlands post-completion and therefore expected it would need to harmonise the benefits of both groups of workers; consequently it anticipated higher pension costs in the future and had to factor these into its business plan.

Actuaries advised on the extent of underfunding and this was factored into a renegotiation of the consideration before the deal was concluded.